MAKING THE CONTACT

DR. ROBERT A. RUSSELL

Audio Enlightenment Press

Giving Voice to the Wisdom of the Ages

Printed in the United States of America

First Printing, 2022
ISBN 978-1-941489-86-4

www.RobertARussell.Org

Table of Contents

Robert A. Russell

Foreword

As you study this book, there are two responsibilities you must assume. First, there are certain truths you must consider. Second, there are certain questions you must answer with all honesty.

God can do anything for you that needs to be done. God will do anything for you that you really want Him to do. God will do everything for you that you will permit Him to do. God will actually give you boundless health, supply, peace and happiness if you want these blessings honestly and your faith is strong enough to take them.

The good things of life are not withheld from you because they are impossible of attainment or because life is cruel, but because of the limp and one-sided thinking that short-circuits your good and keeps it from passing into your life. Your failure to be well, prosperous and happy is not due to any failure in God's love and generosity, but is the result of your superficial way of thinking and living. To put it in a few words, you want health, supply, peace and all the other desirable things of life, but you do not want them with your whole heart and mind. You only think you want them, or you want them to appear without effort on your part. You are unwilling to accept the responsibility of freedom from all kinds of limitation, or perhaps you do not know the Truth. Jesus said, *Ye shall know the truth, and the truth shall make you free.*

Do you really want to be healed of your difficulty? Do you really want to be better? Do you really want to know the Truth? You can, you know, if you are willing to pay the price in mental and spiritual coin.

Robert A. Russell

v

Robert A. Russell

I TOUCH THE HEM OF HIS GARMENT

By Muriel Taylor

I touch the hem of His garment
    Through the crowded cares that press,
Obscuring the Christ within me,
    Who waits as of old to bless.

And I only need to touch Him
    With faith of a bygone day
To find my sins, my errors,
    All wiped away.

I touch the hem of His garment
    Though His presence be unseen,
And my sins are all discarded
    As though they had never been.

I touch the hem of His garment
    And feel His life flow free
Through every cell of my being,
    Renewing me.

I touch the hem of His garment,
    And my spirit is infused
With strength from His life outflowing.
    With joy from His love unloosed.

His virtue I feel within me,
    His wisdom and power revealed.
I touch the hem of His garment
    And I am healed.

Chapter I

Contact Through Christ

And an highway shall be there, and a way, and it shall be called The way of holiness.

Are you sick? Is your body uncomfortable and perhaps racked with pain? Is some organ diseased or out of place or not functioning properly? Are you suffering from some inaction or overaction? Is your mind distressed? Is your spirit rebellious? Do you wonder why God allows such conditions to exist or why He does not answer your prayer? Many persons have asked these same questions and wondered about these same things. But wondering does not get one anywhere.

The question is, What are you going to do about your problem? What would you give to have perfect health in your body and a continuous stream of prosperity in your affairs? What would you give to have power instead of weakness, ease instead of disease, comfort instead of pain, happiness instead of misery, plenty instead of limitation, freedom instead of bondage?

Now answer this question honestly. What *would* you give to have perfect health instead of sickness? Do you say that you would give all the money you possess? Well, maybe you would, but money is not enough. There are lots of things money cannot buy and one of them is health. Health like all other spiritual attributes is a state of mind and must be earned with mental and spiritual coin, by giving yourself, body, mind and spirit to Him, You must deserve it before you can have it. Jesus said, *Work out your own salvation.*

1

Oh, yes, you like to fool yourself and drift along in the assumption that because you are good, respectable and moral, and because you go to church and say your prayers and have a good practitioner that God will save you from whatever you need to be saved from. It is so much easier to think about the Truth and to talk about It than to work It out in your daily life. It is so easy to claim your perfection as a child of God with words and so hard to think always of yourself in terms of perfection and to act accordingly. St. James said, *Be ye doers of the word, and not hearers only, deceiving your own selves.*

Is it a sick body that is torturing you? Then you can be healed spiritually only by putting your life (your mind, your soul and your body) completely under the influence of Jesus Christ and by keeping it there. The indispensable requirement of getting what you want is a deep sense of union with the Power of God. If you have this, you can face your problems and conquer them. If you have this, you can overcome any obstacle in your life. Nothing will be too difficult for you to achieve. If you do not have it, you are wasting your time.

Perhaps the first step in spiritual healing is to make a fresh contact with God. If you want electric power, light or heat, you must turn on the switch. You must tune in to or make some contact with the source of power at the power house. If you want more health, more supply or more of the other good things of life, you must make your contact with the Source of All-Good, the Divine Power House (Christ Consciousness) from which *every good gift and every perfect gift* comes. To complete the circuit is to have all the electricity you need or can use. To be one with the Power of God is to have all good things given to you automatically and to know that they will come as long as you sustain contact with God.

What is it that makes you sick, poor or unhappy? Is it God? Do these negative conditions come from God? Certainly not. Then where do they come from? There is only one place they can come from, and that is from the things in your nature and in your thinking that are ungodlike. There is but one remedy and that lies in getting back to God, in getting a fresh contact with Christ. There is no other way.

The lesson we all need to learn in extricating ourselves from our difficulties is the lesson of putting first things first. *Thou shalt have no other Gods before ME. Look unto ME, and be ye saved, all the ends of the earth; for I AM God, and there is none else. Come unto ME. all ye that labour and are heavy laden, and I will give you rest. I AM the light of the world: he that followeth ME shall not walk in darkness, but shall have the light of life.*

Whoever contacts *ME* (the Christ) will find healing, supply, happiness and peace. When you contact water, you get wet. When you contact electrical power, you get a shock. When you contact the Christ, you partake of His Perfection and His Wholeness. His Life becomes your life. His Mind becomes your mind. His Health becomes your health. His Peace becomes your peace. Job says: *Acquaint now thyself with him, and be at peace: thereby good shall come unto thee. Receive, I pray thee, the law from his mouth, and lay up his words in thine heart.*

Thou shalt make thy prayer unto Him, and thou shalt also decree a thing, and it shall be established unto thee: and the light shall shine upon thy ways.

When you are in the Kingdom of God, you cannot be separated from the things of God's Kingdom. *It is your Father's good pleasure to give you the kingdom.* God's Kingdom is your kingdom; the things that are in it are your things. When you have the mind *which was also in Christ Jesus,* you cannot think or act differently from Christ. To be one with Christ in your thinking is to have the same thinking that Christ has, to have the same power He has and to do the same things He does.

The straight and narrow way of coming into God's Kingdom is through the Mind of Christ. The invitation is clear. *Look unto ME. Come unto ME.* But who is this *ME?* It is God. It is the Father. It is the Christ of Jesus. The *ME* of Jesus is your *ME.* It is everybody's *ME.* When you contact this *ME,* the Christ within you, you contact the Universal *ME,* which is God. The Psalmist sang, *The Lord said unto my Lord.* God turns to you as you turn to God. If you turn only part way, He turns only part way.

But how do you make this contact? By living and thinking under laws of God, not by wordy prayers and petitions or by reading books or listening to sermons and lectures. By bringing your life, body, soul and spirit to Christ and by accepting yourself as you are—a Spiritual Being in a Spiritual World.

Making the contact with God (Universal *ME*) is pretty much like dialing in to a desired station on the radio. There is just one place on the dial at which you can make the contact with the station you desire. There is just one point from which you can get perfect reception. If you touch that point, you get the program desired. If you do not touch it, you do not receive what you are seeking. All around the dial there are other stations broadcasting all sorts of things that you do not wish to hear; it takes careful dialing to avoid undesirable programs and to bring in the right station.

When you accept the invitation to *Come unto ME,* you must by careful selectivity dial into the Christ. You must be determined to know nothing and to practice nothing but the Presence of God. You must see God only in yourself, God only in every person, place and thing. You must have the single eye and the one-pointed mind. *I am God, and there is none else.* In the center of your dial is God, or the Universal *ME,* and all around this Central Station there are the many fictitious broadcasts of disease, sickness, poverty, death, unhappiness and sorrow. St. Paul said, *Stand fast therefore in the liberty wherewith Christ has made us free, and be not entangled again with the yoke of bondage.* To stand fast means to keep dialed to God, to keep the mind stayed on Truth. If you wobble in the process, you will become entangled in the meshes of the human mind. The whole problem revolves around your ability to tune in to the *ME* and to stay tuned in. *He will keep him in perfect peace, whose mind is stayed on thee.* Jesus was a past master in controlling His thought. He gave us the way to tune in to the good things of God's Kingdom when He said, *If ye abide in me, ye shall ask what ye will, and it shall be done unto you.* Nothing is so important in spiritual work as the dialing process. When you tune in to Christ and stay tuned in, you tune out everything that is unlike Christ. Only the God can then get into your life.

This tuning-in process is very well illustrated in the story of the healing of the woman with the issue of blood, told in the Gospels of St. Mark, 5:25-34 and St. Luke, 8:43-48.

The setting of the story is in the crowded ways of an Eastern city. In all old oriental towns, the streets are very narrow. They are much like our modern alleys. A comparatively small gathering of people makes quite a crowd. Jesus accompanied by His disciples is on the way to the bedside of Jairus' daughter who has already been reported dead. There is a crisis and the

Master is on His way to meet it. He walks swiftly: the divine Light is on His face. The healing Power is gathering in His Consciousness ready to go forth in His word for the healing of the young girl. His fame as a healer is so widely known throughout the country that His way is blocked by throngs of people who wish to see Him. Naturally there is great curiosity, and everybody strives for just a glimpse of the man who by his spoken word can cleanse lepers, raise the dead and open the eyes of the blind.

But Jairus, the girl's father, is there, too. With anguish in his soul, he urges Jesus toward his house. His daughter is very low if not even now dead, and his distress is acute. Even the slightest delay seems to him insupportable. There is also in the crowd a great host of Jairus' friends, following to see whether Jesus is able to do another mighty work. They, no doubt, sympathize heartily with Jairus, who is not only a father in deep distress but a man of importance among them. There is too that small group of disciples around their Master striving to keep the people from crowding too closely around Him.

But there is another person of importance in this crowd. Over against the throng of people crowding about Jesus, there is a solitary woman who is so outstanding she will live long in memory. She has no close friends or relatives to bring her to Jesus or to state her case for her. Her condition is distressing and pathetic. For twelve long years she has suffered from an exhausting physical trouble. Doctors can do nothing for her, and she has drained all her available resources, save the one great resource of immortal faith. Her money is gone, for she has spend all her living in seeking health; she now has, in addition to her physical weakness, the mental torture of wondering how she is going to make both ends meet. One cannot imagine a more distressing and hopeless situation, for in addition to twelve years of uniform disappointment and the loss of her money she is considered by the law of Moses unclean. By ceremonial law, she has no business to be in the crowd.

Who is this woman? Her identity is unimportant, but it is important to know what is happening to her and to draw some lesson from her experience. In her extremity a new light has sprung up in her soul. She has heard the things concerning Jesus. She has heard how the sick of Gennesaret have been brought to Him and have been healed. She cannot herself ask permission to be taken to Jesus because of her disability. The great press of the throng makes it impossible for her to attract the attention of the Man of Galilee. There is but one course open to her and she takes it.

She pushes through the crowd, driven by the force of the great idea that has awakened a marvelous hope in her breast. She will be healed and she knows it. There is no doubt in her mind about it. Hers is no idle curiosity to see the miracle worker about whom everybody is talking. Her mission is an all consuming passion. She has a concrete desire and faith that it will be fulfilled that very day. Onward they go, the woman pushing and edging her way nearer and nearer, all the time watching stealthily for her opportunity. Finally the great moment comes. She is near enough. Stooping down suddenly, she touches the hem of Christ's robe, and her bleeding stops. Instantly she is conscious that she is healed.

To the amazement of the crowd, Jesus halts the procession and asks who has touched Him. One of the disciples who has not noticed the woman replies simply that many in the crown have pushed against Him. The reply does not satisfy Jesus, for He knows that a real transference of Power has been made. He knows that this is not a chance contact but that some person with a definite intention has sought divine help and has been healed. He turns around and again asks, *Who touched me?* St. Peter and the disciples gently point out the apparent absurdity of the question. *Master, the multitudes press thee and crush thee.* Jesus knows that he has has a patient who still needs help and that she takes precedence even over Jairus' dying child. He again presses the question, *Who touched me?*

After a moment's delay, in great dismay the woman steps forth. It is an embarrassing and tense moment, for the woman not only has to admit the action which ceremoniously incorrect, but she has to face the indignation of the crowd for hindering Jesus at a very critical time. Again there is but one course open to her and she takes it. *The woman fearing and trembling, knowing what was done in her, came and fell down before him, and told him all the truth.*

A deathlike silence now fills the air. A curious multitude waits with hushed and breathless expectation. The Lord of Life and Ruler of Death is about to make one of the mightiest declarations of all time. He is about to give the key not only to this woman's healing but to the fulfillment of all human desires. Addressing the woman who has just made her confession, Jesus says, *Daughter, be of good comfort: thy faith hath made thee whole.*

John Garner Banks says in *The Healing Evangel,* "If anybody advances the statement that it was not the woman's faith but the healing power of Christ that affected the cure, let me remind you that on the same assumption all of us should be well and whole, for the Will of God is ever for our complete mental and physical and spiritual health; but to give effect to this beneficent purpose, the cooperation of the human will is an imperative necessity, in order that the circuit may be established and that the current of power may flow freely from the divine Dynamo over the wires of faith (or, better, the wireless vibrations of faith) to the waiting needs of humanity."

Is this the end of our story? No. it is only the beginning. It will be finished in you and in every person who takes Christ at His word and touches His seamless robe. The woman has long since passed from this life, Jairus and the disciples have gone, but the story of her faith and its results have come down to us as a promise. It is a promise that most truly will be fulfilled in the life of every person who here and now will meet the conditions and make the contact she made.

Perhaps you are wishing that you too might approach Jesus as this poor woman did and receive healing. You can if you will approach His mystical Body in the same manner as the woman with the issue of blood approached His physical body. The physical body of Jesus disappeared from the earth some two thousand years ago, but He still walks with us and is very near us in His Spiritual Body, which is inherent in very man.

It was not the physical body of Jesus nor was it His garment that healed the woman. It was the Spirit, or Christ, in Jesus. St. Mark says, *She felt in her body that she was healed.* The implication here is that the healing power of Christ which went forth with such suddenness and swiftness was embodied or absorbed by the soul of the woman. Her act of faith was followed instantly by a reflex healing action in her body.

"It is a well know fact in modern psychology that all thought processes are motor in their effects upon the body and faith is a peculiarly dynamic form of thought process. The inference is very clear; if we would experience wholeness of body we must establish right relations with God so that it is possible for our souls and bodies to be oriented towards Him. The right relationship is quite sufficient in the majority of cases to bring about what is called 'Physical Wholeness' though there may be circumstances in the life of the individual which will retard the perfect physical expression of health."*

To be healed in the truest sense involves a bringing of the entire body, soul and mind into perfect harmony with the Mind and Will of God. To be saved in the fullest sense there must be a joint healing of body, soul and mind. The Life Abundant which was transmitted from the indwelling Christ Body during the early ministry of Jesus is available to us today. The same power emanating from the same Source is potentially available to any one who makes the same contact, who brings his body, soul and mind completely under His influence.

He that raised up Christ from the dead shall also quicken your mortal bodies by his Spirit that dwelleth in you. You, too, can touch the hem of our Lord's garment in your mind and be healed, just as was the woman in our story. How are you to know that this is true? Because God has promised that it shall be and because many persons have done it. *As many as touched him were made whole.* All that is required of you is that you stretch forth your hand and touch the Christ with the faith and belief that His power will operate for you as it did for the woman with the issue of blood.

The manner or your approach will, of course, be different, but the process and effect will be the same. You will not actually reach out and touch the physical body of Jesus, but you will contact Him by harmonizing your mind with His. As you

---

* John Gayner Banks in *The Healing Evangel.*

devoutly enter the Body of Christ (His Consciousness), the Christ Spirit, which is germinally within you, will arise in your consciousness and save you from whatever you need to be saved from. He will not only restore you to your true nature as a son of God, but will, if you abide in Him, render your body immune to sickness and disease.

Be ye transformed by the renewing of your mind. It makes no difference whether you contact your Christ symbolically, metaphysically or intuitively, or whether you touch Him in the Sacrament of Holy Communion as you receive the sacred elements and hear the transforming words, "Preserve thy body and soul . . ." or whether you touch Him in the Silence by conscious realization of His Indwelling Presence.

> "The healing of His seamless dress
> Is by our beds of pain;
> We touch Him in life's throng and press
> And we are whole again." — *Whittier.*

Robert A. Russell

Chapter II

Contact Through Consciousness

You can touch His Seamless Robe and be healed of all your difficulties—

> *Because you have the same God He had—the God who forgiveth all thine iniquities; who healeth all thy diseases; who redeemeth thy life from destruction.*

> *Because you have the same Christ He had—the Christ who shall change our . . . body, that it may be fashioned like unto his glorious body, according to the working whereby he is able even to subdue all things unto himself.*

> *Because you have the same Faith He had—the faith that is the substance of things hoped for, the evidence of things not seen.*

> *Because you have the same Mind He had—the Mind that will transform you by the renewing of your mind.*

> *Because you have the same Word He had—the Word that shall not return . . . void.*

> *Because you have the same Power He had—the Power that is able to do exceeding abundantly above all that you ask or think.*

The thing that fascinates most people in our story is the outer or material robe which Jesus wore. This was probably woven of white lamb's wool and was seamless from top to bottom.

Such a robe was of course a badge of distinction in those days and a mark of wealth. It was only natural that Jesus, the master of all Supply, would wear the very best. We would not expect Him to do otherwise. But we have dwelt too much on the material garment and not enough on the mental garment that was His real robe.

His real robe was a mental garment, spoken of in metaphysics as the aura, or outer extension of Consciousness. In the Bible *it is referred to as the wedding garment and the armour of God.* The theologian speaks of it as a non-atomic enswathement of immortal Spirit. The terms are unimportant. In plain everyday speech, the aura is the mental or thought atmosphere that a person carries about with him constantly. It is the direct result of all that he has every thought, said or done; it decides what is to take place in his life; it attracts what is like itself and repels what is unlike. When Jesus said, *Come unto ME,* he was speaking of His Consciousness. There was no power to heal the woman in the robe that Jesus wore. The power came through His Consciousness. She touched His Consciousness by reaching out to Him.

St. Paul said, *There is a natural body and there is a spiritual body.* It may surprise you to be told that right here and now you have two bodies instead of one, that in addition to the physical body which you see when you peer into the looking glass, you have also another very substantial but invisible etheric body, which is the same shape as your physical body and interpenetrates it as water does a sponge.

It is hard to describe the auric body expect to say it is the repository of all your thoughts and feelings, that it is made up of several different densities of ether and that it extends beyond the physical body. It surrounds the wearer in some cases like a dark pall, and in others like a brilliant white light. With those who are negative in thought, it is so shriveled and contracted that it hugs the wearer tightly. With those who are spiritually conscious, it may extend beyond the body several feet.

There are some people who claim they can see the auric body; but as a rule, it is not something that is seen but something that is felt. In some mysterious manner the quality of this robe in every person is sensed by others. It is the great radiating center of the mind; it publishes to the world what is in the consciousness.

Many poets and writers have tried to describe the aura of Jesus, but we can only imagine what it was like. He had a perfect consciousness of the Presence of God. He was aware every instant of the transforming Power within Him upon which He could call at any time for anything He needed. His God was a living Reality permeating His whole Being and radiating from Him as a tremendous, quickening Power. Artists have tried to picture this spiritual radiation by painting a halo of light above His head, but in reality it surrounded Him completely and extended from His body no one knows how far. We can only imagine the wonder and beauty of the true robe, invisible, transcendent and all-powerful.

The brilliant, penetrative power and perfection of His Consciousness is shown in the statement that His robe was seamless. That is, there were no breaks in the continuity of the fabric. It was woven from top to bottom without seams, thus typifying the purity and perfection of the Consciousness He had attained. Being without seam, His robe was faultless. There was nothing in Him for evil to work with. When the woman reached to touch the robe that Jesus wore, she touched

His consciousness and the power of that contact flooded her body with instant healing.

Jesus Christ is still here, a glorious, vital, living reality. He is here as Omnipresent Spirit. Did He not say, *I go to prepare a place for you, that where I am, there ye may be also, and Lo, I am with you always?* When Jesus left the earth, He simply went from the here into the everywhere. Why did He do this? So he could make His Spirit (Consciousness) instantly available to all men no matter where they were. He went away that He might come again with greater accessibility, power and glory. *God is a Spirit and they that worship him must worship him in spirit and in truth.* It is no longer necessary to hunt for Him in Galilee or Jerusalem. Look for Him in your own mind and heart and you will find Him there.

Has His departure in any way changed His availability, helpfulness and power or our relationship to Him? Not at all. Jesus was never so far from His disciples as when He walked with them in the flesh. It was only when He was no more seen by them that He became an intimate and living Reality to their souls. Our present contact can be even more direct, intimate and full than it would have been when Jesus was here in the flesh. The only difference in getting to the Master is in our approach. Instead of looking to the physical personality of Jesus as in the days of old, we look to the Christ within us — the Christ who is as near to us as our inmost thought about Him.

Wherefore henceforth know we no man after the flesh; yea though we have known Christ after the flesh, yet now we know him no more.

Yes, the Christ still walks among us, though unseen, and we can still touch the hem of His garment if we understand that it is His Presence we are touching. How do we touch Him? Through recognition, faith, affirmation and realization. St. Paul said, *Our citizenship is in Heaven.* Where is Heaven? Jesus answers, *The kingdom of God is within you* [within your own consciousness]. The way to God is through your Christ. Spiritual healing is not a matter of substituting one body for another body, but of releasing the Christ Body. Its Powers and Virtues are inherent within the physical body. It is already there in embryo; It needs only to be recognized and realized in order to materialize in experience.

Note the tense of our text, *Our citizenship is* [not *shall be*] *in Heaven.* Right now the mystic Christ within is waiting to be recognized, longing to build us up, to clothe us with new bodies, *like unto His glorious body.*

When St. Paul said, *Let this mind be in you which was also in Christ Jesus,* he was telling us to be filled with the consciousness of Christ's Presence. To be filled with His Presence is, of course, putting on the whole robe. In the beginning, it is not necessary to put on the whole garment in order to obtain help. We need only to contact the garment, for it is so powerful that even the slightest touch will bring instant relief from suffering.

But no one should stop with a partial putting-on of the robe. The imperious command is to *Put on the whole armour of God.* The more fully you are aware of His Presence, the greater your power and ability become. You do not need to touch any man or woman in the outer; you do not need to beg, beseech or implore God to give you something that is already yours.

The seamless robe is within the sanctuary of our own heart; you must seek it there if you are to find it. There and there

---

* American Standard Version of the Bible.

only can you make a quick contact with the Christ and be saved from whatever you need to be saved from. If your mind is filled with the consciousness of His Presence and your faith firmly fixed in the Christ, like the woman in our story you need only to touch the hem of His garment to find the things you seek.

There is a very important point in this story that must not be overlooked. The crowd was the great obstacle that stood between the woman and Jesus. To most sick women this would have been a formidable barrier. To reach Jesus was not an easy task, but her faith and certainty in the outcome of her contact was so strong that nothing could hold her back. There was only one way to get through to Him and that was to push her way through. It was, according to human sense, impossible for her to get through. She could not get to Jesus, but she did. In spite of the ridicule that the crowd heaped upon her, she didn't give up for an instant. Her determination to reach Christ was so strong that it carried her triumphantly to her goal in spite of all interference.

Do you wonder what all this has to do with you? As you seek healing, you will find, like this woman, that your way will seem blocked at times by a crowd of negative thoughts, doubts and fears. Just when you are about to reach your goal, some suggestion from doctor or friend, some fear or discouragement will creep in, and you will lose heart. You will perhaps be told that there is no hope, or that your case is incurable. New symptoms may appear, and your trouble may seem to be worse. Do not pay attention to such negations, but press onward. Was the woman deterred by twelve years' failure to be healed or by the angry glances of the crowd she pushed aside in getting to her Lord that day? Not at all. She had but one idea and that was to be healed. She disregarded everything else and pushed on.

The two lessons every Truth student must learn are fixity of vision (the ability to look through the crowd to Christ) and singleness of purpose. If you have these qualities, you will succeed; if you do not have them, you will fail. Every negative thought and suggestion that stand in your way must be pushed aside to make way for the Christ. Every paralyzing fear, suggestion and false appearance must be ignored. Every thought of discouragement must be stamped out. *Power belongeth unto God,* said St. Paul. *Look unto ME and be ye saved.* Do not argue with symptoms or with disease. Do not talk back to illness and dignify it in any way. See only your perfection and wholeness, and your perseverence will enable you to overcome your difficulty just as the woman did.

If thine eye be single, thy whole body shall be full of light. You do not have to demonstrate healing, abundance or anything else you desire. They are already demonstrated for you. All you have to do is to accept them under the Laws of God. How do you do that? By rejecting everything that is inimical to the Kingdom of God. The Christ is with you now. His seamless robe is within your reach. All you need is the faith and the courage to stretch forth your mind toward the Christ, and, keeping it stayed on Him, disregard all the hindrances and obstacles in your path.

The command, *Prepare ye the way of the Lord,* indicates that there are obstructions to be removed. You will meet plenty of them, as everybody does, but if your mind is filled with the Presence of God, you will override them and come victoriously to your goal. Armed with perseverance, you will succeed in the face of the most trying and hopeless circumstances. Acknowledge Him and He will give you the desires of your heart. To make quick contact with Christ, you must never think or speak that which is contrary to the Truth. You must not pay any attention to time, discouragement or to anything else in the relative world. Jesus said, *To this end was I born, and for this cause came I into the world, that I should bear witness unto the truth.* This is a good rule of life, for every follower of Christ is properly self-governed only when he allows the Power to use him.

And the government shall be upon his shoulder. God has endowed you with certain inalienable rights among which are self-government and the ability to think what you want to think and to say what you want to say. There is only one person in the world who can get you to admit that you are sick, and that person is yourself. The Christ cannot direct you to think the Truth. He said, *I go unto my Father.* If you allow yourself to think and talk disease, sickness and poverty, you are going away from the Father and not with Him. You are automatically cutting yourself off from Supply and dethroning yourself. Remember that it is the practice of Truth and not the profession that brings the blessing.

Lo, I am with you always. The Christ Consciousness is everywhere. It covers the earth. Power is all around you, and it is only necessary to let it flow like a mighty river. When the contact is made, the result will show in the physical man. Healing will begin at once. Before you know it, you will be whole and well. Moses said, *It shall come to pass if thou shalt hearken diligently unto the voice of the Lord thy God, to observe and to do all his commandments which I command thee this day, that the Lord thy God will set thee on high above all nations of the earth: and these blessing shall come on thee and overtake thee, if thou shalt hearken unto the voice of the Lord thy God.* The Power will never fail you if you trust It and give yourself to It. You must keep your mind moving with the Power. You must keep it moving toward health by keeping it closed to sickness.

Does all this sound incredible to you and too good to be true? You can test it by putting it to work in your life. *Prove me now herewith, saith the Lord of Hosts, and see if I will not open you the windows of Heaven, and pour you out such blessing, that there shall not be room enough to receive it.* Like everything Jesus taught, these ideas need only to be put to work to prove their worth. All that you need in order to prove God is faith and the willingness to let the Christ Consciousness take possession of you.

You have tried other things. Why not try Christ? Touch the hem of His seamless robe and be healed of every trouble. *In your patience ye shall win your souls.** When you feel discouraged or are about to sell out to evil, remember that the potentiality of one is the potentiality of all. What thousands have done, you can do. If you have the determination and perseverance and steadfast faith, you can overcome anything in your life. You can be healed of any disease; you can solve any problem. Having His Mind in you, you can wear His robe and do the things that He did.

No man can be more acutely aware of the problems of humanity than a clergyman whose life has been devoted to the healing ministry of the Christian church. After twenty-five years' experience in dealing with thousands of cases of every manner and kind, I offer as my humble judgment that the one thing America desperately needs today is a new and more intimate relationship with God. The world is full of people who live for the day alone, who attempt to find satisfaction in the pleasure of the moment, who are content with the temporary aspect of things and do not look beyond it. When trouble comes, however, when this intensely personal world begins to fall apart, the man who does not recognize a Power greater than himself is like a ship without a rudder in a storm-

---

* American Standard Version of the Bible.

21

tossed sea. He is at the mercy of chance and of public opinion. His confidence in himself gone, he distrusts everyone.

He has cut himself off from the Divine Circuit, has become a detached, isolated unit, open to all manner of disintegration, barrenness, infirmity and disease. In this detached state, he is like a stagnant pool by the roadside, cut off from the Great Source and River of Life, becoming in time a festering place where only disease, misery and limitation can grow.

There are countless millions of unsatisfied people whose lives are out of balance and who, deep in their souls, are unhappy because the spiritual part of their natures is undeveloped and they are frustrated by life. Even greater numbers suffering from inner conflicts are always at war within themselves. They, too, are sick. They do not sleep soundly at night. They do not digest their food properly. Their days are inwardly frantic. They have no peace within themselves.

Physicians and psychologists the world over bear witness to man's need of religion.

Dr. C. G. Jung, eminent Swiss physician and psychologist, says, "I should like to call attention to the fact that among my patients over thirty years of age there has not been one whose problem in the last resort was not that of finding a religious outlook on life. It is safe to say that everyone of them fell ill because he had lost that which living religion bestows, and none of them had been really healed who did not regain his religious outlook."

Dr. Alexis Carrel in *Man the Unknown* states that there is much deeper relationship between psychological and even physiological processes and the spiritual life than we have supposed. Indeed, he assumes an advanced position by describing with apparent approval the recorded healings at Lourdes, and declares on the basis of these cures that "the only condition indispensable to the phenomenon [of healing] is prayer."

He gives the further interesting suggestion that "there is no need for the patient himself to pray . . . it is sufficient that someone around him be in a state of prayer." In all healing he regards prayer as of profound importance but warns, and wisely, that prayer should not be understood as a mere mechanical recitation of formulas but as absorption of the consciousness in God. He defines prayer as man offering himself to God. A man standing before God is as the canvas standing before the painter, "I am empty; fill me as you will," and the artist fills the canvas full of his own genius. Taking this attitude toward the Power of God, any sufferer is bound to find new strength and healing.

Dr. John Rathbone Oliver, professor of medicine at Johns Hopkins university, declares that the greatest psychologist or healer who every lived is Jesus of Nazareth. "Nowadays," he says, "I sometimes hear one of my psychiatric colleagues proclaiming some new truth in connection with mental illness, and somehow the new doctrine seems to have a familiar sound. When I trace this familiarity to its source, I find myself not in the latest books by Freud or Adler, but in the Gospels. Many principles that our Lord laid down long ago have been rediscovered by scientists and proclaimed from the housetops as something new."

During His brief ministry in the flesh, Jesus often referred to Himself as a physician. Whenever He finished speaking, great crowds pressed upon Him *and sought to touch him, for there went virtue out of him and healed them all.* Since by His own word, this great Power is still available and operative, and as millions and millions who have been healed spiritually will testify, anybody who completely opens himself, body, mind and spirit, to the influence and power of God will straightway become a channel through which this divine power will flow. It means that he will be healed of everything that needs healing. With this thought in mind, Emerson said, "Let us take our bloated nothingness out of the way of the divine circuits."

Dr. J. A. Hadfield, the eminent neurologist of Oxford, says the greatest psychologist tend toward the view that the fundamental source of power is to be regarded as some impulse that works through us and is not of our making. Bergson speaks of it as the *elan vital.* Janet refers to it as the mental energy. Jung speaks of it as the libido, or urge, a force which surges through our lives.

These are just different ways of saying that you are intended to be a channel of Divine Energy and not merely a receptacle or terminal.

The healing power of the Christian religion and the ability to master sickness through contact with the seamless robe are not set forth in this book as theory but as fact. It has been demonstrated time and time again that no matter what the disease if a person will fulfill the condition of healing by adopting the attitude of a little child and surrendering himself to God, he will be saved from whatever he needs to be saved from.

Chapter III

Contact Through Mind

Let this Mind be in you, which was also in Christ Jesus.

Be ye transformed by the renewing of your mind.

The connecting link between God and man is Mind. God is Mind. You are mind. Your consciousness is made up of Mind and it's ideas, and these ideas determine whether you are healthy or sick, prosperous or poor. To contact God and bring forth Good, you must study Mind and Its laws. To know god as your health, you must learn how to give health to your mind and how to make Truth and not physical appearance the base of your every thought. *Hitherto have ye asked nothing in my name: ask and ye shall receive, that your joy may be full.* What does it mean to ask in His Name? What is the Nature of God? God is Mind. To ask in His Nature is to ask in His Mind. St. Paul said, *Let this mind be in you, which was also in Christ Jesus.*

There are three phases of Mind; God Mind, Christ Mind and the human mind. The Great Mind is God symbolized as the Father. It is the embodiment of everything in the universe. The Christ Mind, the link between man and God, is symbolized as the Son, the Only Begotten Son. The Christ Mind is both conscious of God and conscious of you. It is that which brings you and God together. The third phase of Mind is the human mind, by which you can employ the Christ Mind and the God Mind to supply your needs and fulfill your desires, or by which you can deprive or limit yourself of these blessings. If

25

you think and live solely by the limited power of your human mind, you are running on one cylinder and living in darkness. You are not only depriving yourself of the good things of life, but what is worse, you are bringing evil and unhappiness into your experience.

Whatsoever ye shall ask in my name, that will I do. When we ask in His Name, all three phases of Mind operate as One Mind, and the answer will come.

Your mind, not knowing what you use it for and not caring, will work from any model you furnish it. Divine Mind responds to you by corresponding to your states of thought. If you hold steadfastly before your mind the idea of the Perfect Christ Body which is inherently within you and believe in its realization, it will transform and renew your outer body in accordance with this mental pattern you have given it. Your body, being the effect or form of your thinking, will be healed only as your thought is healed. You will glorify God in your body only as you drop from your mind all ungodlike thoughts and beliefs.

Naturally, the desire of the average sick person is to be healed. Such a desire is both natural and reasonable. The possibility of healing is inherently within the mind of every living soul. The demonstration of healing comes as the individual consciously yields the three phases of being, boy, soul and mind, to God. The body is restored to its perfect state when the beliefs and thoughts which created the short circuits in the first place are displaced by Truth.

Mental displacement is a process of surrender. The way of break a negative belief is to form a positive one. You break the evil belief by cutting off its food supply, by refusing to exercise it, and then you fill the mind full of something better. If you are to be *transformed by the renewing of your mind,* the whole mind must be geared to new ways of thinking, new impulses, new ideas and new ideals. You must cut off everything that has fed the old beliefs in the past. You must disassociate yourself from every idea that has stimulated the old beliefs and take into your mind spiritual ideas and impulses that move with God. When you know with your whole mind that one with God is a majority, you can assume a lofty indifference to worry, fear, sickness and all the myriad false beliefs that keep millions in bondage to evil. You can say to the biggest challenge, "So what?" and mean it because you see through it to Reality.

I pray God your whole spirit and soul and body be preserved blameless. Spiritual healing according to St. Paul is a joint healing of body, soul and spirit. Since the body is the result of the physical, mental and spiritual activity that goes on within a man's being, the healthiest person is the one who maintains a true balance. Jesus said, *Be ye therefore perfect, even as your Father which is in heaven is perfect.* Perfection is attained and normal functions restored only as body, soul and spirit operate as one.

Spiritual healing does not begin with symptoms, diagnosis, paralyzed limbs, sightless eyes and diseased organs. These are changeable and unsubstantial appearances. "Substance [body] is plastic and Spirit [Mind] is compelling" is an old metaphysical truism. Spiritual healing begins with the breaking up of the imperfect images that have caused the conditions of sickness. It begins when the enervating habits of thinking and living that have been building disease are broken. The key to spiritual healing is self-control, both mental and physical. In the physical realm, nature must be given a chance to eliminate the accumulated poison from the system. In the mental realm, God must be given supremacy in thought.

Keep thy heart [subconscious mind] *with all diligence; for out of it are the issues of life.* "The subconscious mind governs the body, for every phase of its development, whether physical, mental or spiritual, has passed through the subconscious through the consciousness or awareness of the individual. An impression received and recorded enters the subconscious a a belief, and from that moment, it proceeds to exercise dominion. We see then how necessary it is to know the Truth and to train the consciousness to allow no unchallenged thought to enter its realm.

"The body of man is an effect, a manifestation of all that he has believed about it, an outcome of his consciousness, as externalization of the idea that his soul has formed of itself. It is thus a continuous creation of the mind, just as the soul is a perpetual creation of God. It would be foolish to deny the existence of the body, but we know that it has no independent existence. It continually derives its being from the mind. As a body it has neither life nor power. Without the consciousness that is expresses, it could do nothing. But on the other hand, neither could the consciousness become expression without an organism. Mind and body must work together in fulfilling the divine purpose, the manifestation of Infinite Goodness."*

The real change in your body must come through a change in your subconscious thought. Instead of thinking of yourself as a destructible, corruptible flesh body subject to pain, sickness and disease, think of yourself as Spirit only. *My son, attend to my words . . . for they are life unto those that find them, and*

---

* Richard Lynch in *Know Thyself.*

health to all their flesh. The actual transformation of mind and body will begin when you withdraw the thought force and substance that have built the condition that you face.

Sickness, like all other errors, has only the power you give it in your thought, feeling, and attention. The thought structure (belief) is the only condition there is and the only substance evil has to feed upon. St. Paul said, *Overcome evil with good.*

Wrong thought structures must be devitalized, demagnetized and dropped out of consciousness. How do you do that? The most effective method is by denial and affirmation. You deny an evil condition by refusing to recognize it, think about it or talk about it, and you substitute the good condition by affirmation, by the recognition and realization of God as the Only Presence and Power. The change that takes place is simply a transference of power from an evil condition to a good condition.

The thing that most people need to do today is to effect a reconciliation between their subconscious minds and their objective minds. What they need is self-control, peace, poise, equanimity, repose. When you send these impulses over the sympathetic nerves to your subconscious maker, you begin to recreate images of a more ideal man, and an approach to Perfection is attained. You must have an ideal, but just having an ideal will not get you anywhere. Your ideal must be lived. If it is for perfect health, you cannot expect negative and sickly states of mind to build it. *Be ye doers of the word, and not hearers only, deceiving your own selves.*

The sins of omission many times are just as disastrous and destructive to the body as the sins of commission. If you do not control your thinking, your emotions and impulses, and live a composed, tranquil, poised and relaxed life, you become tense and build discomfort. You are sick because of wrong thinking and living. Operations simply remove the effect of these. Stop the cause, that is, stop building ill health, and the disease goes away. In the words of Jesus, *Go and sin no more.*

To drop undesirable things out of consciousness may seem difficult, and yet it should be as easy as to drop a burning match from the fingers. The acts of letting-go and of holding-on are both subconscious processes. If you try to let go of things with the conscious mind without giving proper directions to the subconscious mind, you fail. The law says that *If two of you shall agree on earth as touching anything that they shall ask, it shall be done for them of my Father which is in heaven.* Note that word agree. This statement means literally that the conscious and the subconscious minds must be in perfect agreement before the subconscious mind is able to operate.

The conscious mind acts and the subconscious mind reacts. The conscious mind impresses and the subconscious mind expresses. But not every passing thought penetrates to the subconscious. To mesh the conscious and subconscious mind usually requires some feeling. The conscious mind should not try to drive things out of consciousness unless it is in gear. The proper way is to instruct or command the subconscious mind to let go of undesirable thoughts and conditions.

Do not the Scriptures tell you that *The Son of man hath power on earth to forgive sins?* Then exercise your authority and drop from your mind one at a time all the demon structures that have been incubating and generating trouble, sickness, poverty and other perverted conditions in your body and affairs. *Forgive* means to give forth, to get rid of. Say thoughtfully and with deep feeling many times a day, "Subconscious mind of me, by the power of my spiritual word of authority, I command you to LET GO of—(name the belief)." Then know that the subconscious mind is freeing itself. Continue the process until you are free in experience.

Are you weak? Then let go of your weakness and simply touch the hem of Christ's garment of boundless strength. Are you sick in body? Then let go of every thought of sickness and touch the seamless robe of Christ's Life. Feel His healing consciousness flowing into you, cleansing every cell of your body and every negative belief in your mind. Have you a problem? Let go of it. Harmonize your mind with His Mind and the magic touch of His Wisdom will solve it for you and tell you what to do. Are you fearful? Let go of the fear. *Perfect love casteth out fear.* Rest in the knowledge that Christ's Love enfolds you, protects you, upholds you, sustains you and so fills your mind that there is no longer room for fear.

Let go of all little troubles of daily life, the criticisms, vexations and pretty irritations. Don't brood over them and nurse them. Let them go. Let go of the little personal hurts. Let go of worries, envies, jealousies, and hatreds. Sweep them all out of your mind, and you will be surprised at what a renewing effect it will have on your body.

Let go of the big troubles too, the tragic experiences, the terrible disappointments, the deep wrongs, the gross injustices and heart-breaking sorrows. Put away all antagonism and resentment, regret and bitterness. Put away everything that blocks Love, Life and Power. Drop everything that keeps you from living freely, abundantly and fully. Turn to Christ in the midst of you. Touch the hem of His garment and find all that you seek. Rest in the assurance that He will take care of every need, solve every problem and fulfill every desire.

Since Nature renews itself constantly, you can be what you want to be. If you are careful of your thinking, you can use your relationship with Nature to recreate and reconstruct yourself as you ought to be. As God creates the universe by divine ideas, you can recreate your body by your governing and dominating thought. *I die daily,* said St. Paul, and modern science tells you that the physical materials of which your body is composed are constantly changing. Every breath you inhale brings new material. In the course of a few months, you are entirely remade without a single trace of the material that you were once using. You mold the new material by your thought. The body is a tool of your mind.

In Jesus' day, false beliefs and imperfect thought structures were called demons or devils. The word *devil* means divisible and a devil is any false belief in the mind that separates you from your good. The devil is anything that divides your loyalty to God, the Good. The Scriptures tell you that Jesus *suffered not these devils to speak*. If given the opportunity, they will speak through your mouth, through your eyes, your ears, your limbs and through the various other organs of your body. They will tell you how terribly run down you are, how sick and imperfect. They will tell you there is a pain here or there, that the kidneys won't function properly, that the stomach is out of order, that you have a headache, or that you cannot sleep.

What can you do with these devils? Starve them out. Disarm them. Bleed them. *In my name shall they cast out devils.* Every time some little imp jumps into your mind and begins to tell you how terrible you feel and how worried you are, immediately put your mental foot on him and say:

IN THE NAME OF JESUS CHRIST, BE GONE. IN
THE NAME OF JESUS CHRIST OF NAZARETH,

I COMMAND YOU TO COME OUT OF ME. THERE IS ONLY ONE POWER IN MY LIFE, GOD, THE GOOD. I AM A MAN OF AUTHORITY, A MAN OF DOMINION, A MAN AFTER GOD'S IDEA. I AM A SON OF GOD. I REPRESENT GOD IN MY CREATION. MY MIND IS THAT OF PERFECT MAN.

Be emphatic and strong in your exorcism; do not let go until every devil has been cast out.

Not by might, nor by power, but by my Spirit, saith the Lord of Hosts. There are two ways to approach every problem in mind. One is by the might-and-power method of human thinking that gets you nowhere, and the other is by the Christ Mind that always brings success. I the first case, you tackle your problem with the reasoning faculty of the human mind, grimly concentrating all your energy upon the problem's solution. You look at it from every angle and consider it in all its aspects. You wrestle and sweat over it; and then in desperation you wonder if after all you are really solving it. The more you think about it, the more involved it becomes. Finally, like all persons who try to solve their problems by the might-and-power method of the human mind, you give up.

The other way is to recognize that all problems and ills of body and affairs have their origin in your mind and that it is in your own mind that you contact the Christ. You simply relax and, stilling your human mind, you ask Christ to solve the problem for you. There is no strife, struggle nor personal effort in this process. It is a matter of letting-go and letting God do the work. You contact the Divine Presence through stillness, state your problem and ask for wisdom and for the Christ to come to your assistance. Then you wait confidently in silence for the answer to come. The problem will be solved, and with the solution will come a fresh influx of peace, harmony and faith.

Perhaps you get up in the morning feeling rather low. The human mind will at once suggest some medicine, a cathartic or some other material remedy. The might-and-power method is to drug yourself, to take a pill or powder. But the real chemical change must come through the subconscious mind. The spiritual method is to go directly to God, the Great Physician, the Source of all healing. Relaxing in Silence, you touch this inner power with faith. You affirm your oneness and completeness in Him. You try to realize your innate perfection. Presently His Consciousness will pervade your inmost being like a mighty rushing wind. You will be caught up and thrilled with the new sense of power and healing that you feel. Your complaint, whatever it is, is forgotten, gone. You are every whit whole, *Not by might nor power, but by my Spirit.*

But whose looketh into the perfect law of liberty, and continueth therein, he being not a forgetful hearer, but a doer of the work, this man shall be blessed in his dead.

Chapter IV

Contact Through the Word

In the beginning was the word, and the word was with God, and the word was God . . . and without him was not anything made that was made.

Speak the word only and my servant shall be healed.

Your words originate all that happens to you; they are the law unto you. Your words and your thoughts are the source of all your experience. Every belief that you entertain is a mold into which Life pours Substance in a continuous stream.

To contact God through the word there are four steps:

> Speak the Word of Truth.
> Fast from the careless word.
> Feed the Word of Truth.
> From a new mental equivalent.

If you place a glass of muddy water under a faucet so the clear water runs directly into the glass, the constant flow of pure water will clean out the mud. As mud cannot long remain in a glass into which pure water is constantly flowing, sickness and limitation cannot remain in the body and affairs of the one into whose consciousness the Spirit of Truth is constantly flowing. The Word of Truth is comparable to the turning-on of the faucet; under the flow of spiritual Power released by your Word, that which is sick or limited is washed away and body and affairs are filled with health and prosperity. *And the word became flesh, and dwelt among us.*

True and lasting demonstrations of healing are accomplished by consistent right use of your word. True healing comes with the spiritualization and repolarization (redirection) of the mind. It comes with recognition that God is the only Presence and Power in your life and is embodied in you as perfection and wholeness according to your faith. The natural condition of the body is soundness, wholeness and perfection; nature is always on your side to heal, upbuild and recreate. As your word is the instrument that God uses to form substance and to restore and make you whole, your word, rightly formed and spoken, will bring forth whatever you need. *So shall my word be that goeth forth out of my mouth; it shall not return to me void, but shall accomplish that which I please, and it shall prosper in the thing whereunto I sent it.*

If you hold popcorn over an intense flame, it becomes so filled with heat that it suddenly bursts into a new pattern. So it is with your word. Once you unite yourself with God Power, healing takes place. It is as natural as the bursting of the popcorn into its new pattern. The word spoken out of a God-filled consciousness, the word into which the Christ has entered, has such tremendous power to heal and to bless that it destroys all former limitations. Emerson said the utterance of true ideas by one with a mission causes kings to totter on their thrones.

Jesus said, *The words that I speak unto you, they are spirit, and they are life.* He was speaking of what happens to your words when you are united in mind with God Power. The words that He spoke were creative words so vivified with God's Presence that they demonstrated instantly anything He said. St. Luke says, *They were astonished at his doctrine: for his word was with power.* What does *with power* mean? Does this mean that He had a different kind of word than you have? No, It is not the word that is different but the power within it. Jesus' Mind was united with Divine Mind, and god spoke through His word. You too can speak *with power.*

By thy words thou shalt be justified, and by thy words thou shalt be condemned. Your word always has the exact amount of power your contact with God gives it. It is determined by your consciousness of the Presence and the measure of your belief. God will always give that which you can take and nothing more. The degree of your taking is determined by the degree of your mental acceptance. *As thou hast believed, so be it done unto thee.* The Power of God is unconditioned and unlimited, but if your mental equivalent is only a ten watt variety, He can give you only ten watts of Power. God is Life. God is Mind. God is Power. But Life, Mind and Power have to flow through you to manifest in your life. You do not have to provide the Power, but you do have to provide the belief through which the Power is to flow, the mental equivalent upon which it is to act. It is always the belief that attracts the condition necessary for the fulfillment of the thought. Things not just happen to you. It is the Law of Mind that nothing can happen to you, either good or bad, that is not first accepted as a belief in your own consciousness. Would you speak words with power? Then give spiritual words place in your mind. Make room for them.

Lucius Humphrey says, "To perceive an idea, to grasp it, to hold it and use it, continues to be the rule for successful accomplishment." Ernest Holmes says, "As water will freeze into the form that is poured so substance will solidify only into the form that our thought takes." Jesus said, *Keep my word.* To *keep* a word means to hold it in your mind by recognition and realization until it manifests in your life. To keep a word, you must meditate upon it, revolve it in the mind, go over it in all its aspects and believe in it as Truth until it forms in you a consciousness of itself. St. Paul said, *Let Christ* [Truth] *be formed in you.*

Just as the soil holds the seed from which a beautiful flower or a great tree springs, so must you hold the word of Truth in your mind until the embodied idea appears in your experience. To hold the word of Truth, you must give yourself to the Truth that it represents. You must speak it aloud and in the Silence until the very ether and substance of your body vibrate with it. Then you touch the seamless robe and find healing.

Jesus said, *If ye abide in me, and my words abide in you, ye shall ask what ye will, and it shall be done unto you.* It is the holding of the word in mind that unites the human consciousness with the Christ Consciousness and gives you the power to demonstrate over the adverse condition in your life. It is the holding of the word in mind that gives you the power to demonstrate whatever you need or desire. When the human mind, the Christ Mind and the God Mind are perfectly synchronized, then and only then do your thoughts and words become alive with power and produce results according to their nature.

Can you implement this process? Yes, by giving Spirit to the thoughts you think and to the words you speak. How do you do that? By thinking living thought. By giving depth of life and feeling to every thought. Feel the Christ Presence in your thought. Charge your thought with interest and deep feeling just as you charge your automobile battery with electricity. Keep repeating your word. Affirm it often. God will fill it with His Power, and the results will astonish you. If it is health you want, impress this divine state of being deeply upon your subconscious mind. Think of yourself as being strong, healthy and well. Think of yourself as growing in strength and health constantly.

The second step in the process of contacting God through the word is fasting. That is, abstaining from using negative words. Just as a good gardener will keep his seed free from weeds, a good Truth student will keep his mental garden free from all negative thought structures. He will put out of his mind all the beliefs that bind him to old conditions. All the imperfect thoughts that caused the unpleasant conditions and all those that resist and oppose the Truth must be starved out. They must be dropped out of consciousness by refusing to give them attention of any kind. If you are to touch the seamless robe through your word, like the woman in the story, you must push aside all negative and ungodlike ideas. You must push through all inhibitions, doubts, fears and worries and fix your vision steadfastly upon the Christ.

To many persons, fasting from false beliefs and words is mental drudgery, but no other practice pays such large dividends. When you set out to bring into manifestation some new experience, the important thing is to guard yourself against a thought of the opposite nature. Why? Because the opposite thought may entirely neutralize the desired images, or, at least, weaken it. If your words are to be swift and strong and to infuse the divine Energy of God into your Mind, they must be free from all encumbrances. The author of Hebrews said, *Let us lay aside every weight and the sin which doth so easily beset us.* A divided word cannot product positive results.

The third step in contacting God through the word is to feed your Word of Truth, to feed it to the bursting point. Make your word so vital, so strong, so big and so important that it takes up all the space in your consciousness. The command is to *Occupy till I come.* Since it is the subconscious state of your thought that determines what is going to happen to you, you must hold your word until you know it with both the conscious and subconscious minds. You must hold it until thinking the Truth becomes the ruling habit.

To *occupy* till He comes means you must know only God and His ever-present goodness—God only in man, God only in your consciousness, God only in your emotions, God only in your body, God only in your bank account, God only in your home; God only in your friends and relatives and in every stranger. *Occupy till I come* means that you see God and God only in every person, place and thing. It is not God and sickness, but God only. It is not God and poverty, but God only. It is not God and the problems but God only. Omnipresence means All Presence and All Presence means God only, God everywhere.

One of the causes for failures in spiritual demonstration is that the demonstrator does not hold and hew to the line. He divides his attention. He judges according to appearances. St. James says of such a one: *He that wavereth is like a wave of the sea, driven with the wind and tossed; let not that man think that he shall receive anything from the Lord.* You see and think with God only when you give every ounce of your thought substance to omnipresent Good.

The fourth and most important action is building a new mental equivalent. What is a mental equivalent: It is a vehicle or pattern for thought. It is an image, belief or embodiment within yourself of the thing you are asking for. Jesus said, *Whatsoever things ye desire when ye pray, believe that ye have received them and ye shall have them.* When you pray, believe. In other words, ask for what you believe you have instead of asking for what you believe you do not have. The belief is not only the mental equivalent but the guarantee of the thing you are asking for. Without the belief or mental equivalent, your prayer will avail nothing. It doesn't make any difference where you go or what you do, you will never attract anything to yourself but that which you have in your thought. Heaven and hell are within your thought, and they will go with you wherever you go. *The law of the Lord is perfect,* but it always works the way you use it. It works through your beliefs, thoughts and words. God responds to you by corresponding to your states of thought and your mental equivalents.

To make a demonstration, you must first have a mental equivalent of the thing you want to demonstrate. It must be formed within you by desire, affirmation and realization. *If I may but touch the hem of his garment, I shall be whole* was the mental equivalent of the woman who sought Jesus. The supreme moment to demonstrate the Truth is that moment when things on the outside look the worst. The greatest rewards often come in the midst of the greatest difficulties. Mind, however, will always evolve your concepts exactly as you involve them.

The former things have passed away; behold, I make all things new. Note the order of this statement: the old things pass away first and then new things take their place. St. Paul said, *Put off the old and put on the new, which is Christ.* The only way to destroy an old wrong thought-pattern is to stop using it and supply its opposite. If you have an inborn hatred of someone, you do not destroy the pattern of hatred by saying, "I am not going to hate him anymore," Say rather, "Christ in me loves him." When you think love instead of hatred, your problem is solved.

If your body is sick and someone asks how you are, you betray your mental equivalent of health by saying, "Not so well," or even, "I am feeling better." Since the Real Man is always well, the scientific answer is, "I am perfect," If you are told, "Do not think of your body," you tend to concentrate your thought on it. But if you are told, "Think of the seamless robe of Jesus," you no longer pay attention to your body but think of that perfect Consciousness in which all healing takes place. You have switched ideas in your mind, and this process is the key to the management of your thinking.

The plan of salvation does not consist of changing one negative thought for another, but in supplanting negative thoughts with constructive thoughts. It is a process of substitution. You let go of the old in order that you may take hold of the new. If you put a coin in the telephone and get a wrong number and then put in another coin to get the right number, the second coin takes the place of the first coin. That is what happens in your consciousness when you substitute one mental equivalent for another.

The kingdom of God [Good], said Jesus, *is within you.* What does *within* mean? It means the belief, image, thought or word. In contradistinction, the *without* means form, effect, experience. For everything in your experience, both good and bad, there is a mental equivalent. *As a man thinketh in his heart, so is he.* If the things that stand about you in form are not to your liking, you can change them by building new mental equivalents. It makes no difference what you wish to demonstrate, it can come to you only through forming the mental equivalent of that thing. First, you destroy the patterns of the undesirable things in your life by non-recognition; then, you build the new mold for the things you really want, and they come into your experience.

The only purpose this book can possibly have for you is to help you change your thought about the unpleasant conditions in your life. When you keep your thought changed, circumstances and conditions will change accordingly. If you want strength, you must stop thinking weakness, vacillation and instability. You must think instead wholeness, peace, harmony and health. If you want supply, you must stop thinking poverty, limitation and scarcity. You must get the habit of thinking of God's munificent riches and unstinted generosity.

There is no hidden secret or magic key to spiritual demonstration, but if you were to ask, "What is the real secret of success in metaphysical work?" the answer would be, "Change your mind and keep it changed." You do not demonstrate new things, new conditions or new circumstances. You demonstrate mental equivalents and nothing else. When you know that the only thing you can demonstrate is a mental equivalent, you will give your attention to your thinking and to nothing else.

Right now, take the biggest problem in your life, the thing that is troubling you most, the thing you have been wanting to get rid of and change your thought about it. If need be, write your problem on paper and go over it in all its aspects and ramifications. On one side of the paper, list all the negative aspects of the problem, and on the other side, change each to the positive aspect. This practice will help you see the scope of the work you have to do in changing your thought. The column of negatives will, of course, represent the things you must cease thinking about, the things that must be ignored and dropped out of your mind. The column of positives will represents the changes that must be made in your thought, the new mental equivalents that you are going to substitute.

Let us suppose your greatest problem for the moment is one of sickness. On one side of your chart, you will list all the thought structures or patterns that enter the present picture. On the other side, you will list the opposite positive thought. Your lists might look like this:

OLD MENTAL EQUIVALENTS	NEW MENTAL EQUIVALENTS
Negative	*Positive*
sickness	health
illness	wholeness
worry	trust
confusion	peace
fear	confidence
disease	ease
discord	harmony
pain	comfort
weakness	strength
imperfection	perfection
waste	supply
inaction, overaction	perfect right action

Be perfectly honest with yourself in this analysis of your thinking. Include in the column of negatives everything that may have a bearing on your illness, such as pride, envy, greed, selfishness, stubbornness, jealousy, vanity, hatred, cynicism, grief, antagonism. Then proceed to nullify the adverse mental states by substituting the opposite states and impressing them deeply on the subconscious mind.

In time this practice will eliminate the tendency to negative thinking and increase the habit of constructive thought. As you change your thought and keep it changed, the tendency toward sickness and disease will decrease and the tendency toward health will increase. The new mental equivalents firmly held in mind will gradually produce more perfect conditions among the physical organs, functions and faculties until the whole tone and condition of the body are changed and transformed.

Be patient and be determined. You will contact the seamless robe only by keeping your thought changed into the new condition. It is the only way to build a new mental equivalent. If you persevere, you will be astonished at the result.

Speak the word only and my servant shall be healed. In speaking the word go back over your chart and determine just what the word is that you need to speak. For every negative condition there is a corresponding positive condition. Find the word that best describes it you.

Suppose one of your negative structures is confusion. Your new word or mental equivalent should be spoken along these lines:

NO NEGATIVE THOUGHT OF CONFUSION CAN WORK IN MY MIND OR BECOME MANIFEST IN MY BODY, FOR I AM THE EVER-RENEWING, EVER UNFOLDING EXPRESSION OF ORDER AND PEACE.

You will note in this affirmation that you have used both negative and positive aspects of this particular problem but have overcome confusion with peace.

If you wish to use a blanket affirmation to cover the entire problem, then use some such statement at this:

THE REJUVENATING POWER OF THE HOLY SPIRIT IS NOW AT WORK IN EVERY CELL AND FIBER OF MY BEING, MAKING MY FLESH PURE, FRESH AND RADIANT WITH DIVINE LIFE AND WHOLENESS.

If your problem is one of waste as indicated on the chart, build a new mental equivalent by this affirmation:

THERE IS NO WASTE OR LACK IN THE EVER CHANGING LIFE OF GOD. THE CHRIST MIND NOW CONSERVES THE LIFE SUBSTANCE IN ME AND DIRECT IT TO BUILD A PURE, INCORRUPTIBLE BODY THAT WILL ENDURE FOREVER.

The important thing to remember about affirmations is that they should be used many times a day and especially at those times when the thought returns to the negative conditions you are trying to change. Affirmations should never become mere repetition. Each one must be said with a deep feeling of the Truth that it represents. Each affirmation must be felt deeply in every fiber of your being.

Remember, too, that affirmations should always be used in the present tense. It is true now. If you are sick and hope to get well only in the future, the subconscious mind can give you nothing in the present. The subconscious mind responds to you by corresponding to your states of thought. The subconscious mind can give you in the present only what you accept for yourself in the present. In Spirit, now is the only time there is. *Now are we the sons of God.* Perceive this fact. Grasp it. Hold it. Make it your own.

A good question frequently asked by Truth students is, "Why is it necessary to use affirmations? If God is good and is everywhere equally present, why is it necessary to declare or affirm the fact?"

There are two reasons why it is necessary to use affirmations: first, the constantly affirmative state of mind furnishes the finest growing conditions for mental seed; second, the student is helped to keep his eye single upon the image of Truth he wishes to realize.

An affirmation scientifically used terminates in realization, and realization culminates in demonstration. An affirmation is a mental equivalent embodying a truth about God expressed in such a way as to convey to the mind the essence of Truth. When the mind feels the soul of the affirmation, the contact has been made, the truth is realized, and you are free. Jesus said, *Somebody hath touched me; for I perceive that virtue is gone out of me.* Whoever touches the *ME* will receive that same virtue.

Robert A. Russell

Chapter V

Contact Through Faith

Faith is an attitude of the whole mind, a confident expectancy connecting the immediate present with the immediate future. It is a certain knowledge or settled feeling about the universe, God and yourself. It is the power by which you touch the seamless robe of Jesus and awaken your own divinity. If you have faith, your thought acts upon God Substance and your word becomes creative. If you do not have faith, your words are like clouds without rain. Faith is essential to success in any field of endeavor.

Spiritual demonstrations depends almost entirely upon the making and maintaining of certain vital contacts between you and God. Prayer, silence and meditation are just different methods of establishing spiritual contact with God. Holy Communion is a sacramental contact. The five senses are the means whereby you contact the whole world in which you live and draw from it the things that you need. You may say, therefore, that your very existence depends upon your contacts. The word *contact,* according to Webster, means to touch. It is the junction or agreement of two conductors though which a current passes. It consists in bringing two unattached forces together in perfect unity. The sense of touch is responsible for the greatest blessings and the worst evils in your experience. What you touch with your mind, you bring into your life.

There are spiritual senses, too, by which you contact the things of God's Kingdom. In spiritual work, a direct and intimate contact with God must be established that will create the reciprocal action that existed between Jesus and the Father. God relates Himself to you as you relate yourself to Him. Spiritual Power doesn't ask what you are going to use It for any more than the creative soil asks what kind of seed you are planting. It simply works the way you use it. God turns to you as you turn to Him. The Spirit is to you what you are to It. *But as many as received him, to them gave he power to become the sons of God.*

Whenever Jesus touched any one, it was not only to rebuke evil and to call forth good in his life but to stimulate his faith. When the leper came to Him, the record tells us that *Jesus put forth his hand and touched him, saying . . . be thou clean.* In the healing of Simon Peter's mother-in-law, Jesus *touched her hand, and the fever left her.* In the raising of Jairus' daughter, *He took her by the hand . . . and she arose straightway.* After the calling of the Twelve, Jesus found Himself surrounded by great throngs of people from all parts of Judea and Jerusalem *which came to hear him and to be healed of their diseases . . . and they were healed. And the whole multitude sought to touch him, for there went virtue out of him, and healed them all.*

Multitudes still throng Him every day in their prayers, silences and meditations, but very few ever really touch Him and draw from Him that virtue which is so constantly poured out to those who contact Him in agreement and faith. It has been estimated that over ninety per cent of those who fail in spiritual work fail because of a lack of faith and because they have not learned that God does nothing for them except that which He can do through them. When you touch the seamless robe of Jesus, you do not touch something that is flat, round, square, soft, hard, dry or wet, but you touch the Presence of God. You feel divine power flowing through you.

The hem of Jesus' garment had no more power to heal than has the statue or sacred relic in a church. It is the quality of the contact or agreement that causes virtue to come forth. It will be done unto you according to your faith. If you seek the seamless robe for its own sake, you will find it and complete the circuit. If you seek it for selfish ends, the circuit will remain broken.

The woman whose healing forms the pattern of this book had exhausted everything but her faith. After twelve years of failure and disappointment, the fait still latent in her soul sprang into spontaneous activity at the approach of Christ and healed her. Faith is the faculty of the mind that can never die. It may become weak and impotent through neglect; it may become temporarily paralyzed through doubt and fear, but faith, like God, is eternal and cannot be destroyed.

The affirmative factor in all healing is faith. If you have the faith of God, you can accomplish anything you set out to do. If you do not have the faith, nothing can be accomplished. A man came to Jesus one day and asked to be healed. The Master replied, *According to your faith be it done unto you.* He did not say that the healing depended upon God or upon Himself, but that it depended upon the man's faith. To the woman in our story, He said, *Thy faith hath made thee whole.*

When ye pray, believe that ye receive. In his diary George Muller wrote, "It is not enough to begin to pray, nor to pray aright; nor is it enough to continue for a time to pray; but we must patiently, believingly continue in prayer unto the end, but we also believe that God does hear us, and will answer our prayers. Most frequently we fail in not continuing in prayer until the blessing is obtained, and in not expecting the blessing. As assuredly as in any individual these various points are found together, so assuredly will answers be granted to his requests. Prayer alone is not enough. We may pray ever so much, yet, if we do not believe that God will give us what we need, we have no reason to expect that we shall receive what we have asked for."

Faith implies expectancy. Expectancy is one of the first steps in releasing the log jam of uncertainty that bewilders you in the face of great problems. Without expectancy, you are like the beggar at the roadside waiting for someone to come along and drop something into your lap. Without expectancy, there is no creative actions or heat in your prayer.

Of all the thousands of people who walked up and down the narrow streets of Jerusalem, it is recorder that just one person touched Jesus. Thousands of people were in daily physical contact with Him but only this one woman touched Him. This is an interesting and significant point because it means that only one person made an agreement with him and had faith and expectancy to back it up.

The woman in the crowd that day had the ability to focus her attention upon Jesus. She was one-pointed. She had a clear idea of what she wanted to do and she adhered to it. *One thing have I desired of the Lord, that will I seek after. Or in the words of St. Paul, This one thing I do. . . . I press towards the mark of the high calling.*

The creative process begins when you say, "Now let this thing be; let it eternalize in fact." Divine Mind then takes up that image and begins to work on it. *Stand still and see the salvation of the Lord.* If you let the image alone and wait in faith, it will at length materialize.

The crucial point in any demonstration is the space between the formation of the image and the realization. You must not change the character of the model that you hold up to Divine Mind by a thought of an opposite nature or by divided faith. If you do, you will ruin the model. Every Truth student must be consistent in his expectations.

It is a fixed law of metaphysics that an idea held firmly in the mind will come into manifestation in the body or the affairs. It will come quickly or slowly, depending on the accuracy of your pattern, the intensity of your faith and your ability to direct all your thoughts and activities toward the one goal.

The great trinity in speedy demonstration is faith, desire and interest. Back of the idea (idea), there must be strong faith. Back the faith, there must be a driving desire. Back of the desire, there must be a strong interest. To bring quick results, you must have the harmonious action of all three. Desire is the driving force back of faith; interest holds the idea to its goal. Without faith, desire and interest are helpless. It is not necessary to outline in making demonstrations. It is only necessary to hold the idea in mind until the subconscious accepts it; the Law will do the rest.

The best definition of faith is found in the Moffatt's translation of the New Testament: *Now faith means that we are confident of what we hope for, convinced of what we don't see.* Faith declares that all things are possible and proceeds to awaken all the powers of the mind top prove it. It increases the capacity to do the very things that faith declares can be done. Faith knows that in God there is abundance of health and that there is Power to bring this perfect health into tangible evidence in every part of the physical body. Faith not only knows this but acts upon itself to bring health into expression.

As a man thinketh in his heart, so is he. As a man thinketh in his head, so he isn't. It makes no difference how good you are in a moral sense, how much you know intellectually or how hard you pray, the answer to your prayers will always be in terms of what you are; that is, what you have in your consciousness. The things that come to you will always be in accord with the inner states of mind. You will demonstrate what you believe and nothing more. If you believe more in health than you do in sickness, health will come to you. If you believe more in sickness than you do in health, then health will stay away. This is the Law, and no amount of praying, begging or beseeching God will change it. Faith is either positive to the good or positive to the evil. There is only one faith; you may use it for good or for evil.

Many students wail, "If I just had more faith!" But there is no such thing as more faith. There is just faith, and you have plenty of it. It is not more faith you need, but a more intelligent use of the faith you already have. If your faith is negative, as is the case with most sick and unsuccessful people, you need to change its polarity. How do you change the polarity of your faith? By changing the habit of your thinking. Instead of dwelling upon negative things, substitute constructive things.

The object in spiritual healing is not to acquire something new, but to learn how to make your common everyday thinking true, positive and wholesome. The body and mind are so closely related that if your habitual thinking were always true and positive, the body would express health continually. When Peter was astonished over the withered fig tree, Jesus said, *Have faith in God.* In other words, change the polarity of your faith. Since your faith is a subconscious faculty, you alone can change it.

Pray without ceasing, said St. Paul. When you have absolute and unquestioning faith in God the Good, it will no longer be necessary for you to pray for things. They will be given to you automatically because of your unvarying faith and trust in God who gives before you ask. To *pray without ceasing* is to have the knowledge that God is Good and that He is manifesting Good in and for you now. In the final analysis, the only failure there can be in spiritual work is doubt of God's ability to do what need to be done.

If you do not know what kind of faith you have, your spontaneous words and thoughts will tell you. It will show in the magnetic field of your aura. Your aura varies in its power of attraction or repulsion according to the movements of your faith. It is your sphere of influence; it changes with kaleidoscopic rapidity according to the changes in your thought. If your faith is positive, you will not admit evil or negatives into your mind. You will know the Truth about every situation. Your thoughts will always be of Good; you will always speak the Good, and you will expect the Good. If on the other hand, you fear, worry and judge according to appearances, if you register evil, limitation, discord, trouble, sickness and disease your negative faith needs changing.

The kind of faith you have is apparent too in the time it takes for the thing you pray for to materialize in your experience.

Eventual demonstration is good but immediate demonstration is better. We pray, *Thy Kingdom come . . . in earth as it is in heaven, and Give us this day our daily bread,* but we do not have the absolute, unbroken recognition of God as the only Presence and Power in our lives. We do not think in accord with Spirit.

The thing that discourages most people in spiritual work is the time element, or space between the prayer and the answer. Still functioning in time, they do not realize that there is no delay in Spirit and that God is always ready. Few people expect immediate results because they do not realize that the fruit is ripe and that the harvest is ready. *Say not ye, There are yet four months, and then cometh the harvest? behold, I say unto you, Lift up your eyes, and look on the fields; for they are white already unto harvest.*

Actually there can be only one reason for delay and failure in demonstration and that is in our faith. We believe in a coming Kingdom rather than a finished Kingdom. We believe the human mind instead of the Christ Mind. The tense of our faith is all wrong. Until we change it, we postpone the reception of our good.

Do we push a button and expect the door bell to ring next week? No. We expect it to ring now. The Word of God is instant and powerful and it works now. The Spirit there is only the ever-present NOW. *Before they call, I will answer.* The answer is ready before we pray. The gift has already been given.

We do not receive the gift in the present, for we still put our faith in growth, anticipation and improvement. We believe that we are getting better, that the condition is improving, or that we are growing more successful. Our ship is always coming in but it never arrives, for we have never taken that trouble to unload the one that is already in port. When we are thinking in accord with Spirit, we affirm that which is already is. The Kingdom of Heaven does not grow. It is finished. "I am well now." "My problem is solved." "I am well now." "My problem is solved." "I am healed now." "I am successful now." "My finances are adjusted satisfactorily now." "My ship is in." When our faith is in Spirit, the objective manifestation will conform to it.

To pray effectively and successfully, we must have faith that the need itself implies the supply and that the thing we are praying for is already done. The Divine Response is always in the present tense. *And straightway he received his sight. Straightway the man was made whole. Straightway his leprosy was cleaned. In the twinkling of an eye* is the manner of His response. No waiting, no postponement, no accumulating, no growth is necessary. In the *now* everything come to life. In the *now* every need is met. In the now every captivity is broken. Do results seem long delayed in your case? Then take stock of the tense of your faith.

Jesus said, *All things whatsoever ye shall ask in prayer, believing, ye shall receive.* The *believing,* however, must extend from the asking to the receiving in an unbroken, unqualified knowing that the work of the Father is already done. You should always expect immediate results when you pray. The immediacy of the answer will depend entirely on the accuracy and continuity of your faith. Like begets like and like attracts like. Each mind pays in its own money. If we think and pray with the human mind we get human results, which include failure, uncertainty and postponement. If we think and pray with the Mind of Christ, we get instant fulfillment. It makes no difference how uniform and perfect our prayer may be, if we lapse again into appearances after the prayer has started its activity, prayer does not get off the ground. The answer will be in terms of the undesirable instead of the desirable. Why? Because our return in thought to outer appearances evidences more faith in the power of appearances than in the power of God. The real and, in fact, the only purpose of silence and prayer is to make the mind more alert and receptive to the good. Every prayer is answered, as St. James says, but it cannot be answered in terms of our desires until everything of an opposite nature is removed from our thought. In other words, the mind and the prayer must go in the same direction.

First the blade, then the ear, then the full grain in the ear. If we follow this outline when we pray, we can be sure of right results. We can approach God with the same confidence and assurance that we approach the multiplication table and get the same accurate results. Prayer is an exact science, but like every other science it has its conditions. If we pray in the present, laying aside all thought of time, God will become immediately active for us and we bring forth complete, perfect and immediate results.

If the subconscious mind has gotten into a rut, it must be lifted out and reeducated. It must be made to hold the perfect image so firmly that finally it becomes the ruling habit of your life. *Let Christ* [Truth] *be formed in you.* You will touch the hem of His garment only as you impress the True Idea upon your subconscious mind. The realization will come finally through meditation and surrender of self. It will come through the recognition that *In him we live and move and have our being.*

Tell your subconscious mind over and over until the Truth in the statement becomes the frame of reference for every thought and feeling action, "Christ lives in me and manifest His Perfect Being."

Speak the words aloud. Touch them with your faith. Sing them into your work. Meditate on the thought. Revolve it in your mind. Involve it. *Give and it shall be given unto you.* What you give to your subconscious mind will be given back to you in form. What you impress upon it will be expressed in your experience. What you think into it, you express in your body.

And Jesus said, *Somebody hath touched me; for he perceived that virtue had gone out of him.* Whoever touches the Christ Consciousness will know that the *virtue* has come into his keeping. He will feel a strange new power. He will realize that whatever he touches in the subconscious mind will come forth as the fulfillment of what he asks. *If two of you shall agree on earth as touching anything that they shall ask, it shall be done for them.* The sense of touch when freed from the material attachment extends right into the heart of God. Perfect health already exists within you, but you must call it forth by the touch stones of agreement and faith. The agreement is made the conscious and the subconscious minds are perfectly synchronized, that is, when you believe with the whole mind.

Health and disease are both contagious. They respond to your touch (belief). You touch then through your thought and both come readily at your call. If you think sickness, describe symptoms or negative feelings or concentrate upon, adverse condition, you are touching trouble. You are calling upon disease. Of course, it comes because you have touched it with your thought. It is the nature of everything respond to thought. The subconscious mind is a magnet, drawing good and evil in our lives. You draw to yourself whatever corresponds to the negative, you draw negative things. If your faith is positive, you draw constructive things. Whatever you draw is of the nature of your thinking.

The promise is, *In due season ye shall reap, if ye faint not.* It is not uncommon for students to say, "I have tried and I cannot demonstrate." You are demonstrating all the time. You may not like the demonstrations nevertheless. An experience of sickness is just as much a demonstration as an experience of health. They are results of different ways of using faith. Since it is impossible for anyone to be neutral, that is, to shut off this thinking powers altogether, he is demonstrating every moment. Indeed you cannot help demonstrating. The way to change your demonstrations if they are not your liking is to change the polarity of your faith. When your faith is positive and constructive, you automatically touch Good and call It forth.

But to return to the formula, *If two of you agree on earth as touching anything that they shall ask, it shall be done for them.* Now ask yourself if your faith is the perfect agreement with your desire. Do you and your prayers move in the same direction? Have you pushed aside all the piled up human beliefs of sickness, worry, anxiety? Are you observing all the common sense rules of health in eating, resting, sleeping? If you can answer these questions in the affirmative, you deserve to be healed, you can stretch forth your hand to touch His seamless robe.

Now enter the Silence. Let go of everything in the human mind and touch the hem of His garment with these words:

> I AM NOW TOUCHING THE SEAMLESS ROBE OF JESUS AND I AM FREED FROM ALL FALSE BELIEFS IN SICKNESS AND LIMITATION. MY FAITH IN HIM HAS QUICKENED AND RESTORED ME. I OPEN MY MIND TO THE CHRIST CONSCIOUSNESS. THE PURE LIFE AND SUBSTANCE OF GOD FLOWS THROUGH EVERY ATOM OF MY BEING.

Make this contact in the Silence every morning when you awake and each night before you go to sleep. You will be astonished at the changes that take place in your life. Old conditions, worries, fears and antagonisms will drop away from you and blessings will come in every increasing amounts.

From the Silence springs new life and power, but practicing the Silence should not be confined to isolate meditations. It must become an attitude of life. It is possible in the flash of an eye or quicker than thought to establish contact with Spirit to right wrong thinking, to secure physical or mental healing, to renew strength. The awareness of the thinker that he is working on the spiritual plane, his conviction that Truth is the only power, his realization of his Oneness with God are essential factors in securing results. The Silence can be observed in a crowded street, in the midst, at a time of personal crisis. All it requires is withdrawal to the *secret place*.

The poet, Tennyson, very happily expressed this thought:

"Speak to Him thou for her hears and
    Spirit with Spirit can meet—
Closer is He than breathing and
    nearer than hands and feet."

The Lord is in his holy temple: let all the earth keep silence before him. In this inmost place God and man meet, and heaven and earth conjoin in our being. It is a place of stillness and power, of healing and rest. God is in this place: His Presence fills it. It is the Christ center of consciousness—the power-house of God.

Be still and know that I am God. Centered in God's stillness, we set in motion the invisible forces of Good. When we mind the body are absolutely still, we receive the quickening touch of His power. We are drawn up to the height of Christ Consciousness in which we can say, *I live; yet not I, but Christ liveth in me.* We touch the hem of His garment, and the power of our own Christhood is revealed. We are made whole.

The Place of Stillness is not in some distant heaven. It is right where we are at the present moment. We enter into It in such degree as we comprehend and contemplate It.

Within every problem, within every worry and fear, there is a place of quiet and peace. It is like the calm in the center of the storm. God's peace is available to all. *If I ascend up into heaven, though art there: if I make my bed in hell, behold thou art there.* The Silence is all about us; It is the very air we breathe. We can enter It whenever we shut the door of the senses and consciously make the contact with God.

Jesus said, *When thou prayest, enter into thy closet, and when thou hast shut the door, pray to thy Father which is in secret. To touch the peace of God which passeth all understanding,* the human mind and material sense must be mute. Peace does not come to us while our consciousness are filled with all the little importuning thoughts and problems of the human mind nor while we are busy arranging and expressing all the ideas and impressions already within us. Face your problem before you enter the Silence if you must, but do not take it with you when you enter. The command is to *Stand still and see the salvation of the Lord.* As thought and feeling are withdrawn from the outer world, as we listen for the Voice of Truth, we are lifted into the realm of the Spirit, and we touch the peace of God.

My soul, wait thou only upon God; for my expectation is from him. Whenever we touch the peace of God, His Presence comes forth in outward expression. It comes forth as new understanding and power. We see with the inner eye. Obstacles become stepping stones, discord becomes harmony, sickness becomes health.

In the true sense, Silence is communion with God. It is the merging of the human mind with the Divine Mind. The word *communion* means literally to be on common ground, to be in a state of equality. In the Silence, we are aware that we are one with the Father, and He is one with us. The power of His Spirit is released through our consciousness.

There is a technique, an habitual approach, through which you can train or educate the objective mind. You must first learn to relax your body. Routine is more readily established if the time and place of your observation of the Silence are kept the same. Remove all sights that might distract you, eliminate all disturbing elements in advance, make yourself as comfortable as possible.

Concentrate your thought upon a metaphysical truth, a Scriptural quotation, or a word that is meaningful or peculiarly significant to you at the moment. Consider it from every angle. Enlarge upon it in your thought. Hold it until the meaning takes possession of you.

As you meditate, see the word in action in your life and in the lives of those about you. Claims its power for yourself and for all men. Listen for the Voice. Be grateful for your awareness of your Oneness with God.

Be sure that your specific need or desire is spiritually legal (that is, it can harm no one) and translate it into terms of its spiritual equivalent. Then realize that it is already in fulfillment. *Before they call, I will answer.* Your need has been met, your problem solved, your desire granted. Do not attempt to outline the way in which this is to come about, for *Eye hath not seen, nor ear heard, nor have entered into the heart of man, the things which God hath prepared for them that love him. Close with the thought,*

Father, I thank thee, that thou hast heard me. Then go on your way with a new sense of security and peace.

This is a very brief summary of the steps in the Silence.* You will find much in print concerning the subject which will prove to you that there is no set pattern. Each person must find his own way. You will eventually find yours, and it may not be like that of any other person. Your ideal will be, of course, to live in It, to follow habitually the injunction in the words: *Whatsoever things are true, whatsoever things are honest, whatsoever things are just, whatsoever things are pure, whatsoever things are lovely, whatsoever things are of good report . . . think on these things, for As a man thinketh in his heart, so is he.*

It is perfectly possible for a man to starve to death with his pockets full of money if he does not know that it has purchasing power. One stands helpless before a locked door if he does not have a key. The key to the door to the abundant life is awareness of your place in creation. *Son, thou art with me always and all that I have is thine,* said the father to the prodigal son. Jesus said, *It is your Father's good pleasure to give you the kingdom and the kingdom of God is within you.*

Consider too these statements:

I am the Lord in the midst of the earth.

The Lord is in the midst of thee: thou shalt not see evil any more.

The Lord in the midst of thee is mighty.

The mystery that hath been hid from ages and from generations but now made manifest . . . which is Christ in you.

---

* See God Works Through Silence.

He that dwelleth in the secret place of the most High shall abide under the shadow of the Almighty.

Lo; I come, and I will dwell in the midst of thee, saith the Lord.

The Lord is at hand.

But you may be aware and still not profit. The key must be used. Like the woman who touched the robe, you must use your awareness, your faith, your belief to make the contact with God, with Life, Truth, Love, Power, Intelligence. You must accept your own divinity and that of every other person. The first words of the Lord's Prayer establish all humanity as one: *Our Father.* Until you see the divinity in your fellow-man, you have not claimed your won. Until you can see through the evidence of the senses and discern the Real Man in your neighbor, you have not taken possession of the Kingdom of God despite the fact that It is within you. Divine Sonship means awakening to the Real Self, coming to terms with It, letting It think and act for you. *Now are we the sons of God.*

Before Abraham was, I am. The Father of lights with whom is no variableness, neither shadow of turning. The knowledge that we cannot change God in this contact we seek leads to a feeling of satisfaction. In the Scriptures, He is declared to be Omnipotent, Glorious, Long-Suffering, Eternal, Compassionate, Righteous, Upright, Immutable, Omniscient, Omnipresent, Incorruptible, Faithful, Immortal; and His attributes are defined as Knowledge, Wisdom, Power, Truth, Goodness, Mercy and Love.

Who would want to change Him? With David, he can say:

OF OLD HAST THOU LAID THE FOUNDATIONS OF THE EARTH: AND THE HEAVENS ARE THE

WORK OF THY HANDS. THEY SHALL PERISH, BUT THOU SHALT ENDURE: YEA, ALL OF THEM SHALL WAX OLD LIKE A GARMENT; AS A VESTURE SHALL THOU CHANGE THEM, AND THEY SHALL BE CHANGED. BUT THOU ART THE SAME, AND THY YEARS SHALL HAVE NO END.

The change must come within us. Our prayers, thoughts, words are only for the purpose of establishing ourselves in our own minds as outlets of His Good. As an arm of the sea, a gulf, a bay or an inlet, no matter how small, partakes of the nature of the Ocean itself, so we by the awareness of our Oneness with Him share His Powers and Attributes.

When we are transformed by the renewing of spirit, express our strength in improved human relationships and in every other aspect of our environment. Seeing with new eyes, we change our experience, for it is always determined by the inner vision. We realize that health is not merely the restoration of movement to a reluctant limb or the creation of harmony in the disturbed digestion but Wholeness in mind and body. The "grasshopper thoughts" *(We were in our own sight as grasshoppers, and so were we in theirs.)* give place to the new Consciousness of Oneness. We see prosperity not as a matter of things we own, cars, bank accounts, real estate, but a means to greater freedom, increased livingness and fuller expression of life, and we measure it in terms of confidence, contentment, achievement, security and joy.

Now turn back to the Foreword. Have you seriously considered the Truth as it appears on these pages? Have you honestly answered the questions raised? Are you ready now to recognize that your life is what you have made it, that it is the result of the consciousness you have developed? Are you willing to pay in spiritual coin to change that consciousness, to elevate it, to unify it with the Christ Consciousness?

If your answer is yes, if you have stretched forth your hand to touch Him, His words are spoken as directly to you today as to the woman in the long ago.

BE OF GOOD COMFORT; THY FAITH HATH MADE THEE WHOLE; GO IN PEACE.

Robert A. Russell

Acknowledgment

In the making of any book, the author finds himself under obligation to many persons. There are those who have contributed ideas, and there are others whose words are remembered when their source is forgotten or impossible to identify. The appreciation of the writer of this book is no less sincere because of the impossibility of making public acknowledgment of their service. Direct quotations in this book are credited to their respective authors.

— Robert A. Russell

Raisa - Mystic Alchemist

Energy Healing, Chakra Alignment, Sacred Geometry, Sound Healing

Tammy:

I was blessed with a healing session by Raisa last week. She felt like a friend and like-minded gentle soul with comforting Mother Mary essence pouring through her words. Raisa was so in-tuned to my blocks and traumas held within my field. She used her connection to ascended masters I've resonated with such as Yeshua, Mother Mary, Mary Magdalene, Lady Vesta & Amethyst and archangels Metatron, Michael and others to help clear these.

I was able to address childhood trauma situations to flip the stuck energy I've held onto over the years. She also picked up on a few traumatic past-life scenes that have affected my current life. I am an intuitive energy healer who truly felt the shift and healing within. I now feel so much lighter and have clarity regarding my path.

So much love and gratitude to you both, Raisa and Barry for presenting her to my world! (More Testimonials on following Pages)

Contact Raisa to book an Energy Healing
or Chakra Alignment session:
www.RaisinYourIsness.com
raisinyourisness@hotmail.com

Shannon:

This BEAUTIFUL sister...our Raisa... is a treasure beyond compare! After my experience in my personal session with Raisa... the ABSOLUTE confirmation I received, that could ONLY be confirmed by HER mind you... this session solidified EVERYTHING for me. I KNOW that this sister... she is a formidable, magnificent & IRREPLACEABLE component in this Earth plane story we all are invested in! IF YOU ARE DRAWN TO HER FOLLOW YOUR HEART

No other can do what SHE is gifted to do for YOU... YES YOU!

I LOVE YOU dear sister! I am forever grateful for what only you could do and DID for me! I would have happily paid any price for what you gave me! I URGE YOU ALL to schedule a session with this beloved one!

P.S. thank you Barry for sharing her with us all!

∞

Natasha:

I would like to thank Barry for introducing us to Raisa. I have had 2 consultations with her in the last month and I am in total awe of what transpired. Raisa is such a beautiful caring soul! She connected with me as though she has known me forever. Her love and dedication in assisting others is so touching. I had an amazing experience and some profound healing. I received a message from Jeshua which brought tears to my eyes. I could feel the LOVE in the message that was given to me and I will remember and cherish His message forever. Raisa has really helped me in confronting fears, trauma and past life karma. I have found the reason for my skin problems which I never would have thought it'd be possible. It is amazing what guilt and shame from past lives can actually do to your body. Her healing and that from our Angelic beings has really made a huge difference in my life. I can feel it in my energy. Raisa has a lovely sense of humour, always reminding you not to take life and yourself so seriously. I really feel like a heavy weight has been lifted off my soul. Thank you so much! Much Love!

∞

Ariel:

Raisa... Divine Raisa... You are a Treasure to this Life, and I thank All That Is, and this also Treasured YT channel for the priceless blessing which was our session this AM. Every moment of the session was a fractal explosion of wonderful intuitive & divinely guided perfection. I honor your sincere, caring, graceful, playful, soothing, encouraging, transformational, empowering, and so beautiful demonstration / embodiment of Goddess energy and presence. I am so honored & thankful to have been guided to You. To have invested in the patience, time, energy, and resources to share sacred healing and uplifting time with You. I will remember the session Always. And I will look forward to any and all ways our Creator deems it harmonious to connect again. I could go on and on and on, so please accept my parting acknowledgment of your blessing to this realm, my Heart & Spirt, my Life, and the Lives of all those who may be positively impacted via your assistance. Blessings, and Gratitude, a thousand times over and over again. Namaste... Namaste... Namaste...

∞

B.G.

I have just finished a healing session with Raisa. The experience was remarkable! I am still buzzing! I heard about her from this channel, so thank you deeply Barry!

Raisa is so lovely to talk to, and intuitively guided, knows how to get to the hidden roots of our issues. She calls upon ascended masters, archangels and such to do deep energetic clearing and healing work. It was like being guided through the deep layers of myself, releasing the things that don't serve me and filling every cell with light. I purged, and I absorbed new energy, and came out feeling uplifted and renewed. Raisa helped me to find things in myself that I had been cut off from, and to heal wounds I had tried to bury. She has also given me helpful ideas to continue to improve things my life.

I am so blessed to have found Raisa, and ever grateful for the healing work she has done. She is as authentic as they come. Truly an earth angel! Thank you, thank you, thank you!

YouTube

YouTube Channels of Interest:

Giving Voice to the Wisdom of the Ages

Over 5,000 audios, hundreds of
Spiritual and Metaphysical
audio books including
Robert A Russell, Dr Murdo MacDonald Bayne,
Napoleon Hill, Jeshua, Kryon and many more.

I AM Meditations and Affirmations

Hundreds of I AM Meditations,
Daily affirmations and more.

Raisin' Your Isness

Metaphysical Musings, Channelings,
Sound Healing Songs